Little People, **BIG DREAMS**

ANNE FRANK

Written by
Mª Isabel Sánchez Vegara

Illustrated by
Sveta Dorosheva

Frances Lincoln
Children's Books

Anne was a little Jewish girl who was born in Germany. She lived happily with her parents, and her older sister Margot, in the city of Frankfurt.

Frankfurter Zeitung
HITLER SIEGT!
DEUTSCHLAND
ERWACHE
5 TAGE!!!

But when she was four, an ugly man with a little black moustache became the leader of her country. His name was Hitler. He hated the Jews and wanted them to disappear.

Anne's family moved away to Holland, which was a free country. Anne's father opened a business and they had a home where they felt safe.

But one day, the Nazis invaded half of Europe and arrived in Holland. Anne and all the other Jewish children were forced to go to separate schools and wear a star on their chest.

For her 13th birthday, Anne's parents gave her a diary. That day she discovered the pleasure of writing on her own.

Jhr
Gewicht
kg
109 1101
kg

Anne wrote in her diary about how her family lived in fear of being arrested. They decided to leave their home, and move to a secret annex behind a bookshelf at the building where her father worked.

They had to share their tiny new home with another Jewish family and stay very quiet. They could not leave their hiding place in case anyone found them.

Anne's diary kept her company and she wrote in it for hours. She wanted to publish a book and become a famous writer.

But one day, Anne stopped writing. The Nazi soldiers had found them and they were all arrested. Anne's diary was left behind in her room.

Modes de Paris

The family were pushed onto a train full of people on its way to a concentration camp. It took three long days for them to arrive at the worst place on Earth.

Anne's father, Otto, was the only member of the family to survive the terrible war. He found her diary and wept as he read what his young daughter had written.

ԱՆՆԱ
ՖՐԱՆԿԻ
ՕՐԱԳԻՐԸ
ANNA FRANK
Ana Frank
O Diario de
Anne Frank

He decided to publish the diary, and share Anne's story, just as she would have wanted. The world had to know the true story.

Since then, millions of people have read and cried with *The Diary of Anne Frank*, the story of the little girl who dreamt of a better world.

ANNE FRANK

(Born 1929 • Died 1945)

1931

1935

Annelies Frank was born in Germany to a happy family. But when she was four, a cruel government, called the Nazi party, came into power. It was led by a man named Adolf Hitler, a dictator who forced Germans to follow his unjust rule. The Nazis hated many races, especially Jews, and brought in discriminatory rules against them. Anne's family had to move to Holland in order to be safe. But in 1939, the Nazi party started World War Two, and began invading other countries – including Holland. In 1942 things got worse, and the Frank family had to go into hiding. They hid in a secret annex, tucked behind a bookshelf at Otto Frank's work. They hoped they wouldn't be arrested. Here, Anne kept a diary.

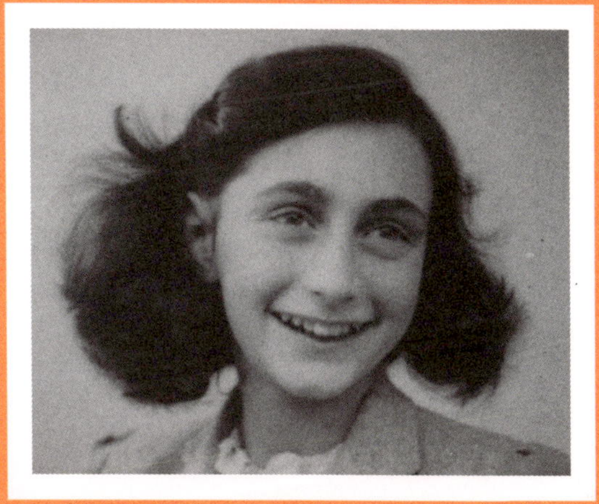

1941

1942

She wanted to tell her story of the war and for people to read it. In 1944, German police broke into the annex and arrested Anne's family. They were all sent to concentration camps. Concentration camps were prisons where many Jews were forced to work. There was little food, lots of people, and disease spread quickly. Most people did not survive. Anne died at the Bergen-Belsen camp in 1945, weeks before it was freed by allied forces. After the war, Otto found her diary and published her story, as she would have wanted. Anne became one of the most loved diarists in the world, and captured the hearts and minds of the public. She lives on through her words and in all those who read her story.

Want to find out more about **Anne Frank?**
Have a read of these great books:

The Diary of a Young Girl by Anne Frank
Who Was Anne Frank? by Ann Abramson and Nancy Harrison
Famous People Famous Lives: Anne Frank by Harriet Castor
DK: The Story of Anne Frank by Brenda Ralph Lewis

If you're in Amsterdam, you could even visit the Anne Frank Museum – where Anne lived in secret and wrote her diary.

First Published in the UK in 2018 by Frances Lincoln Children's Books, an imprint of The Quarto Group.
The Old Brewery, 6 Blundell Street, London N7 9BH, United Kingdom.
T (0)20 7700 6700 F (0)20 7700 8066 **www.QuartoKnows.com**
First Published in Spain in 2018 under the title Pequeña & Grande Anne Frank
by Alba Editorial, s.l.u., Baixada de Sant Miquel, 1, 08002 Barcelona
www.albaeditorial.es

Published by arrangement with Alba Editorial, s.l.u. Translation rights arranged by IMC Agència Literària, SL

A catalogue record for this book is available from the British Library.
ISBN 978-1-78603-292-8

The illustrations were created by hand with nib pen and ink, and watercolour. Set in Futura BT.

Published by Rachel Williams • Designed by Karissa Santos
Edited by Katy Flint • Production by Jenny Cundill

Manufactured in Guangdong, China CC092019

9 7 5 3 1 2 4 6 8

Photographic acknowledgements (pages 28-29, from left to right) 1. Anne Frank at Two, 1931 © Anne Frank Fonds Basel / Getty Images 2. Anne in Switzerland, 1935 © Anne Frank Fonds Basel / Getty Images 3. Anne Frank, 1941 © Anne Frank Fonds Basel / Getty Images 4. Anne Frank, 1942, Photo Collection Anne Frank House, Amsterdam, Public Domain Work

FSC www.fsc.org
MIX
Paper from responsible sources
FSC® C008047

Collect the *Little People,* **BIG DREAMS** series:

FRIDA KAHLO

ISBN: 978-1-84780-770-0

COCO CHANEL

ISBN: 978-1-84780-771-7

MAYA ANGELOU

ISBN: 978-1-84780-890-5

AMELIA EARHART

ISBN: 978-1-84780-885-1

AGATHA CHRISTIE

ISBN: 978-1-84780-959-9

MARIE CURIE

ISBN: 978-1-84780-961-2

ROSA PARKS

ISBN: 978-1-78603-017-7

AUDREY HEPBURN

ISBN: 978-1-78603-052-8

EMMELINE PANKHURST

ISBN: 978-1-78603-019-1

ELLA FITZGERALD

ISBN: 978-1-78603-086-3

ADA LOVELACE

ISBN: 978-1-78603-075-7

JANE AUSTEN

ISBN: 978-1-78603-119-8

GEORGIA O'KEEFFE

ISBN: 978-1-78603-121-1

HARRIET TUBMAN

ISBN: 978-1-78603-289-8

ANNE FRANK

ISBN: 978-1-78603-292-8

MOTHER TERESA

ISBN: 978-1-78603-290-4

JOSEPHINE BAKER

ISBN: 978-1-78603-291-1

L. M. MONTGOMERY

ISBN: 978-1-78603-295-9

JANE GOODALL

ISBN: 978-1-78603-294-2

SIMONE DE BEAUVOIR

ISBN: 978-1-78603-293-5

Now in board book format:

COCO CHANEL

ISBN: 978-1-78603-246-1

MAYA ANGELOU

ISBN: 978-1-78603-250-8

FRIDA KAHLO

ISBN: 978-1-78603-248-5

AMELIA EARHART

ISBN: 978-1-78603-251-5

MARIE CURIE

ISBN: 978-1-78603-254-6

Little People, **BIG DREAMS**

MAYA ANGELOU

Little People, **BIG DREAMS**

MAYA ANGELOU

Written by
Lisbeth Kaiser

Illustrated by
Leire Salaberria

Frances Lincoln
Children's Books

Marguerite was born in the city of St. Louis, U.S.A. Her brother called her Maya. When Maya was four, she and her brother were sent to live with their grandmother in Stamps, Arkansas.

Growing up in the South, Maya was treated unfairly because of the colour of her skin and because she was a girl. The world outside was very cruel.

OPEN
WHITE ONLY
GENERAL STORE

Home was hard too. When Maya was eight, her mother's boyfriend attacked her. Maya was so upset, she stopped talking.

POEMS OF CABIN AND FIELD
PAUL LAURENCE DUNBAR

A friend of her grandmother's named Mrs Flowers noticed that Maya was afraid to use her voice. Mrs Flowers showed Maya all kinds of wonderful books, and how the words come alive when you read them out loud.

Maya found her voice again in the stories and poems of great writers. She loved words so much, she read every book in the library.

a b c d e
f g h i j
k l m n o
p q r s t
u v w x y z

Even though Maya was a great student, she was told that she couldn't get a good job because of the colour of her skin.

But she had pride and hope. She thought, "There's nothing I can't be."

And she was right.
She was a cook and a streetcar conductor.

She was a dancer, a singer and an actress.

She travelled the world, and learned to speak a lot of languages.

At home in America, she worked to help all people get treated equally.

RIGHTS FOR WOMEN
STOP VIO-LENCE
STOP
STOP

It wasn't until Maya was all grown up that
she decided she wanted to be a writer.
So she began writing a book about her life.

She told the story of a little girl who struggled through hard times but didn't give up.

People all around the world were moved by her powerful story and her beautiful words.

Maya became a famous writer, teacher and speaker, inspiring everyone with her belief that you can be anything you want to be.

On the day Bill Clinton became president, Maya read a poem. She had once been a little girl who was afraid to use her voice. Now she was speaking to the entire country, about her favourite thing: hope.

"Lift up your hearts ...

MAYA ANGELOU

(Born 1928 • Died 2014)

1937

1957

Maya Angelou is one of the most memorable voices in American culture. Born Marguerite Annie Johnson in St. Louis, Missouri, she spent much of her childhood in a small town in the South. There, she faced a lot of unfairness because of her skin colour. When she was eight, she was attacked by her mother's boyfriend and she stopped speaking for five years. In that time, she grew to love books and found power and strength in words. Maya overcame her childhood struggles and went on to lead a marvellous life. She became a dancer, singer, actress, writer, director, journalist, playwright, producer, teacher and an activist

1971

1990

for civil rights. She performed in nightclubs, and began calling herself Maya Angelou. She also became a mother and a grandmother. In 1969, Maya turned the memories from her childhood into a book called *I Know Why the Caged Bird Sings*. The book became famous and sold millions of copies around the world. Maya wrote many more books, won many awards and read her poems at the White House and the United Nations. People everywhere continue to be inspired by her incredible life, her beautiful words and her powerful, hopeful voice.

Want to find out more about **Maya Angelou**?

She has written many great books herself, like:
Poetry for Young People: Maya Angelou edited by Dr. Edwin Graves Wilson Ph.D, illustrated by Jerome Lagarrigue

You could also try these biographies:
Who Was Maya Angelou? by Ellen Labrecque, Dede Putra and Nancy Harrison
Maya Angelou: Journey of the Heart by Jayne Pettit

Quarto Knows

First published in the UK and the US in 2016 by Frances Lincoln Children's Books,
74–77 White Lion Street, London N1 9PF, UK
QuartoKnows.com
Visit our blogs at QuartoKnows.com

Commissioned as part of the Little People, Big Dreams series,
conceived by Mª Isabel Sánchez Vegara.
Originally published under the title Pequeña & Grande by Alba Editorial (www.albaeditorial.es)
Translation rights arranged by IMC Literary Agency

A catalogue record for this book is available from the British Library.

ISBN 978-1-84780-890-5

Manufactured in Guangdong, China CC092019

1 3 5 7 9 8 6 4 2

MIX
Paper from responsible sources
FSC® C008047
FSC www.fsc.org

Photographic acknowledgements (pages 28-29, from left to right) 1. Photo and Maya Angelou™ is a trademark of Caged Bird Legacy, LLC. MayaAngelou.com 2. Photo © Everett Collection Historical / Alamy Stock Photo 3. Photo © ASSOCIATED PRESS 4. Photo by: Universal History Archive/UIG via Getty images

Collect the *Little People*, **BIG DREAMS** series:

FRIDA KAHLO

ISBN: 978-1-84780-770-0

COCO CHANEL

ISBN: 978-1-84780-771-7

MAYA ANGELOU

ISBN: 978-1-84780-890-5

AMELIA EARHART

ISBN: 978-1-84780-885-1

AGATHA CHRISTIE

ISBN: 978-1-84780-959-9

MARIE CURIE

ISBN: 978-1-84780-961-2

ROSA PARKS

ISBN: 978-1-78603-017-7

AUDREY HEPBURN

ISBN: 978-1-78603-052-8

EMMELINE PANKHURST

ISBN: 978-1-78603-019-1

ELLA FITZGERALD

ISBN: 978-1-78603-086-3

ADA LOVELACE

ISBN: 978-1-78603-075-7

JANE AUSTEN

ISBN: 978-1-78603-119-8

GEORGIA O'KEEFFE

ISBN: 978-1-78603-121-1

HARRIET TUBMAN

ISBN: 978-1-78603-289-8

ANNE FRANK

ISBN: 978-1-78603-292-8

MOTHER TERESA

ISBN: 978-1-78603-290-4

JOSEPHINE BAKER

ISBN: 978-1-78603-291-1

L. M. MONTGOMERY

ISBN: 978-1-78603-295-9

JANE GOODALL

ISBN: 978-1-78603-294-2

SIMONE DE BEAUVOIR

ISBN: 978-1-78603-293-5

Now in board book format:

COCO CHANEL

ISBN: 978-1-78603-246-1

MAYA ANGELOU

ISBN: 978-1-78603-250-8

FRIDA KAHLO

ISBN: 978-1-78603-248-5

AMELIA EARHART

ISBN: 978-1-78603-251-5

MARIE CURIE

ISBN: 978-1-78603-254-6

The Austen family lived in the heart of the English countryside. Every evening, there were eight children seated at the table for dinner: James, George, Edward, Henry, Francis, Charles, Cassandra...

Little People, **BIG DREAMS**

JANE AUSTEN

Written by
Mª Isabel Sánchez Vegara

Illustrated by
Katie Wilson

Frances Lincoln
Children's Books

... and little Jane!

At that time, girls were only allowed to do things like singing, sewing and housework. Jane and her sister Cassandra found being a girl a bit of a pain.

However, Jane's father ran a school and taught the sons of wealthy men. One day, he asked his daughters to join their classes and learn the same things as the boys.

Jane loved to read. She always chose a book instead of her dolls and spent endless hours in her parents' library.

Jane and her siblings would often write and perform their own plays. She came up with the best stories and soon realised she wanted to become a writer!

Every night, her seven brothers and sisters sat around the fireplace. They loved listening to Jane's stories until it was time to go to bed.

One evening Jane was at a ball and met a young man named Tom. As they talked, they fell more and more in love with each other.

But Tom's family thought Jane wasn't good enough for their son. And instead of fighting for what he wanted, he proposed to a rich heiress to please his family.

Jane decided to write a similar story to this, but with a much happier ending. And so, the novel *Pride and Prejudice* was born. A daring girl named Lizzy was its heroine.

Jane kept on writing about young women who were brave enough to make their own choices and who never gave up.

MARIANNE
FANNY
ELIZABETH

When her first book came out, many people loved it.
But Jane decided to keep her name a secret.

Jane went on to write seven novels full of grace and talent. Little did she know that, one day, she would be considered one of the greatest writers in the world.

Jane Austen

Little Jane would be happy that the books she once wrote are the ones we still love reading today.

JANE AUSTEN

(Born 1775 • Died 1817)

c. 1788

c. 1810

Jane Austen was born in Steventon, in England. As the seventh of eight children, she grew up in a very large family with six brothers and one sister. She was extremely close to her only sister, Cassandra, for her whole life. Her family valued learning and Jane went to boarding school. She received a limited education but had to return home due to sickness. She was then educated at home by her father. It was in these early years that her love of reading and writing began. She wrote poems, plays and stories, and then her first work, *Love and Friendship*, at the age of 14. It poked fun at the over-dramatic novels that were popular at the

19th century

2017

time and showed her clear talent for language. Jane carried on writing and authored seven very famous novels including: *Sense and Sensibility, Pride and Prejudice, Emma* and *Persuasion.* They all offered witty insights into the lives of the landed gentry at that time. Jane published her books anonymously under the name 'A. Lady' and it wasn't until after her death that she was recognised for her talent. Now, her works are rarely out of print or off the television screen. Although she received a proposal, Jane chose not to marry. She lived a happy life surrounded by family. To this day, she remains one of the world's most beloved writers.

Want to find out more about **Jane Austen?**
Have a read of these great books:

Search and Find: Pride & Prejudice by Sarah Powell and Amanda Enright
Where's Jane? by Rebecca Smith and Katy Dockrill
Who Was Jane Austen? by Sarah Fabiny
Pride and Prejudice retold by Susanna Davidson and Simona Bursi

If you're in England, you could even visit Jane Austen's House Museum – where Jane lived and wrote her bestselling books.

First Published in the UK in 2018 by Lincoln Children's Books, an imprint of The Quarto Group.
The Old Brewery, 6 Blundell Street, London N7 9BH, United Kingdom.
T (0)20 7700 6700 F (0)20 7700 8066 **www.QuartoKnows.com**
First Published in Spain in 2018 under the title Pequeña & Grande Jane Austen
by Alba Editorial, s.l.u., Baixada de Sant Miquel, 1, 08002 Barcelona
www.albaeditorial.es

A catalogue record for this book is available from the British Library.
ISBN 978-1-78603-119-8

The illustrations were created with watercolour, gouache, coloured pencils and digital techniques. Set in Futura BT

Published by Rachel Williams • Designed by Karissa Santos
Edited by Katy Flint • Production by Jenny Cundill

Manufactured in Guangdong, China CC092019

9 8 7 6 5 4 3 2 1

Photographic acknowledgements (pages 28-29, from left to right) 1. Jane Austen – portrait of the English novelist as a young woman, from the painting by Ozias Humphry © Lebrecht Music and Arts Photo Libray / Alamy 2. Jane Austen (1775–1817) pencil and watercolour by her sister, Cassandra Austen, c. 1810 © Granger Historical Picture Archive / Alamy 3. Jane Austen stipple engraving, 19th century © Granger Historical Picture Archive / Alamy 4. The new 2017 Polymer ten pound banknote, 2017 © Malcolm Haines / Alamy

FSC www.fsc.org MIX Paper from responsible sources FSC® C008047

Collect the *Little People,* **BIG DREAMS** series:

FRIDA KAHLO

ISBN: 978-1-84780-770-0

COCO CHANEL

ISBN: 978-1-84780-771-7

MAYA ANGELOU

ISBN: 978-1-84780-890-5

AMELIA EARHART

ISBN: 978-1-84780-885-1

AGATHA CHRISTIE

ISBN: 978-1-84780-959-9

MARIE CURIE

ISBN: 978-1-84780-961-2

ROSA PARKS

ISBN: 978-1-78603-017-7

AUDREY HEPBURN

ISBN: 978-1-78603-052-8

EMMELINE PANKHURST

ISBN: 978-1-78603-019-1

ELLA FITZGERALD

ISBN: 978-1-78603-086-3

ADA LOVELACE

ISBN: 978-1-78603-075-7

JANE AUSTEN

ISBN: 978-1-78603-119-8

GEORGIA O'KEEFFE

ISBN: 978-1-78603-121-1

HARRIET TUBMAN

ISBN: 978-1-78603-289-8

ANNE FRANK

ISBN: 978-1-78603-292-8

MOTHER TERESA

ISBN: 978-1-78603-290-4

JOSEPHINE BAKER

ISBN: 978-1-78603-291-1

L. M. MONTGOMERY

ISBN: 978-1-78603-295-9

JANE GOODALL

ISBN: 978-1-78603-294-2

SIMONE DE BEAUVOIR

ISBN: 978-1-78603-293-5

Now in board book format:

COCO CHANEL

ISBN: 978-1-78603-246-1

MAYA ANGELOU

ISBN: 978-1-78603-250-8

FRIDA KAHLO

ISBN: 978-1-78603-248-5

AMELIA EARHART

ISBN: 978-1-78603-251-5

MARIE CURIE

ISBN: 978-1-78603-254-6